Your Coach
Rules OK

Volume 1

David Holland MBA

Contents

Welcome to my little book of Blogs...

Thinking, Being and Doing Different are probably the key defining success factors in business and in life...

Being positively differentiated from others takes us out of the crowded "red water" and into the clear, open "blue water" of higher margins, service, and value...

So how can this be achieved...?

By being creative and innovative; not doing what others do...

Creativity comes from emotion more than logic, it lives in the abstract world of colour, imagery and metaphor; it strikes us when we are least expecting it and is conjured up in the shower, the theatre or listening to music...

Taking lessons from science, mythology and psychology; even taking lines out of a movie can all be used as fuel to drive our creativity...

For example...

"We have codified our existence to bring it down to human size to make it comprehensible. We've created a scale so that we can forget it's unfathomable scale..."

Quoted from the 2014 Film "Lucy" starring Scarlett Johansson

Seeing how to apply a range of disparate ideas and concepts to business and life success can make the difference between mediocre and amazing, between profit and loss and frustration and happiness…

So this book of blogs takes you on a journey of ideas, thoughts and metaphors that have come to me over the last few years; some will make sense and some will leave you stumped – but I hope you find something you can use and apply to give you that "blue water" experience, create something unique out of nothing and help you on your journey…

Enjoy the read…

Cheers

David

Planning Sucks

March 25th, 2014

...trust your subconscious - *stop thinking so much...*

First of all - lets look at how we drive our cars and use our GPS...

Strange I know - but go with me here, it will make sense...

Let's suppose that I want to drive from Monaco to London. I enter the destination into the GPS and it will calculate a route for me.

It may ask a few questions about avoiding toll roads and ferries, but once it knows where I want to go and how I want to get there, it can give me the advice I need...

Some things that our GPS doesn't do...

1. **Check Your Past** - it doesn't say **"well you were in Berlin yesterday, so you can't be in Monaco now..."** or **"You haven't been to Italy yet so you can't go to London..."** -

these are ridiculous questions and totally irrelevant to the journey.

In Life and Business, however, when we set our Goals and Objectives, sometimes we let a voice in side our head tell us that we are not "ready" or "worthy" yet - or we convince ourselves that because we don't have a Degree, MBA or the right connections we cannot start the journey at all.

2. **Check Your Future** - it doesn't say **"oooohhh, you don't want to go there..."** or **"are you sure, wouldn't you rather go to Paris...?"** The GPS believes what you tell it to be true and behaves accordingly and without question.

Our Subconscious is the same - whatever we tell it, it takes as being true. So whether we tell it positive, negative, inspiring or limiting facts and phrases; it takes them as truth and guides us. It is non-judgmental...

3. **Show a Picture of your Destination** - the GPS does not focus you on the destination. It focuses you on the immediate future and present. The screen image gives you around 200 meters of the road ahead and guides you turn by turn.

Essentially, we have to trust that the GPS will make the right choices for us. If we have to divert off course or avoid an accident or roadworks that it doesn't know about, it will simply re calculate and get us back on track.

This is how our subconscious works too - once we tell it where we want to go, it will guide our actions and decisions to take us there - we have to stop planning so much and start trusting our instinct to make the right choices.

4. **Give In or Tell You Off** - your GPS never gives in, no matter how many times you go off track, make a wrong turn or ignore the instructions, it is there to serve you and look after your interests - same as your subconscious.

   I have tested this out and if I continually ignore the instructions the voice never says "**for #%$@ sake, do what I tell you or else...**" or "**you're an idiot and cant't drive anyway...**" it is non-judgmental and consistent in its manner and emotional state.

   Your subconscious is the same, it doesn't matter how many mistakes you make, or how skilled you are - it will still guide you...

   If you feel like giving in, or listening to other people telling you off, it just means you haven't arrived yet, ignore them and trust your instinct.

5. **Distract You** - once the destination is set, your GPS will only give you instructions that you need, it will go quiet while the road is straight; sometimes no news is good news and it simply means that you are on track, silence is not an opportunity to change direction.

   When we lived in Nevada we could drive across the Desert for hours and not see a soul, the GPS would be silent. Even the view on the screen would be a single vertical blue line through the wilderness - we had to let it do it's job.

   A friend had an App that would chirp in if the GPS was silent, stating for example "**I'm wearing black underwear....**" or "**would you like to do something naughty...?**" - in Life and Business we need to make sure we are not distracted and stay on course...

Applying the Rules to Business and Life...

I have rarely seen a Business Plan that works - what I mean is that usually something happens that wasn't predicted. The biggest challenges and opportunities are those we don't predict - and yet we keep Planning the details and get frustrated when we don't hit the targets...

Stop It...

Here's how to stop **Planning** and start **Achieving**...

1. Set the Objective - the destination, refer to it often but don't keep it as your only focus, the focus has to be the Present, dealing with both the planned and unpredictable as they occur.

2. Ignore the Past - your history need not define your future, unless you let it. If you think you don't deserve, are too young / old, not clever enough - then you are right.

3. Get Moving - if you don't move you will not get anywhere. Procrastinating and Thinking about what to do is the best way of achieving nothing, get on with it and let your instinct guide you.

I had a message from someone who said that they "**had been thinking seriously about working with a Coach for the last three months...**" - not sure what "serious thinking" actually is, but I guarantee it is not helping...

4. Trust - your instinct. Once you have chosen where to go and how to get there, allow your subconscious to do its work; it may seem odd occasionally, but it will be right in the end and get you to your destination safely.

As with the GPS, your journey may be a long one, but your attention should be on the immediate adjustments and turns you make on the way. Essentially it is possible to drive from Monaco to London in steps of 200 meters, that is as far ahead as you need to see.

We always had a Dream of living in rural France, but we had n clue how to make it happen. Our Business took us all over the UK and we eventually ended up living and working out of Las Vegas in the USA; we didn't seem to be getting any closer to our Dream, in fact we were 5,000 miles further away than we were when we started.

However, it was the move to the USA that actually created the opportunity for us to be based out of France - where we are now - joining the dots backwards it all makes sense, at the time, however, it seemed slightly crazy...

We trusted our instincts not our logic - that's what gets results...

So it is with Business and Life;

Long Term **Intention** + *Short Term* **Attention** = **Results**

Because as we know **Results Rules OK...**

PS - If you want to give God a good laugh - *tell her your plans...*

It pays to listen in Bars in Las Vegas

March 26th, 2014

It Shouldn't Happen to a Coach...

...true life stories from our travels through life....

Moving to live in Las Vegas seemed like a bit of fun - *so we sold up and took our business over the Pond...*

I arrived 6 weeks before the family and had to find somewhere to live - didn't realise that Vegas was such a big town...

In the Hotel I was staying in - The Platinum, just off the Strip - I got talking to a guy at the Bar, as one does when in Vegas...

He was in Real Estate, and although originally from the deep south, knew the Las Vegas market well, or so it seemed...

After a few drinks, he decided to give me a piece of advice...

"Whatever you do, make sure you live in a Gay community...!"

Me - "Really...?"

"Yep, you'll be safe there and among likeminded people, away from all the psycho's..."

Me - "I'm married with two kids...."

"Exactly, that's why you need to be in a protected area...."

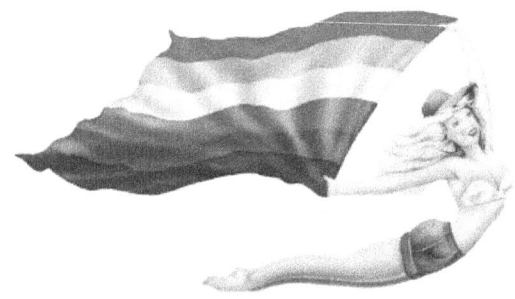

That night I called Lynn and told her what advice I had been given, and that I would go to ReMax in the morning and see what I could find...

As an open / broad minded individual I saw no problem in principle with living in a Gay Community - live and let live and all that...

So off to ReMax I went...

When asked by the assistant if she could be of any help I said yes...

"I need a family size home in a secure Gay community..."

Her - "Really - why...?"

"Well it will be safer there and we will be with other likeminded people away from the psycho's..."

Apparently - *as the conversation developed* - I leaned that there are no Gay communities in Las Vegas and in fact what had been described to me in a broad Southern Drawl was in fact a *Gated Community...*

Doh...!

So off to Summerlin we went - and Slate Harbour Circle was our Las Vegas Home....

Smothered by a Comfort Blanket

April 7th, 2014

How to Succeed in Business

...Why most people never start, or Fail if they do...

John did well at school and went on to get his Degree in Economics from a well-known and highly regarded University in the UK.

By 28 he was married with two children, had a successful career in the Insurance industry and had become a Manager of a small team of brokers specialising in commercial risk in the shipping and international freight market.

With his wife, they bought a house with a mortgage of £300,000, and he had a company Audi A6, with 32 Days holiday and an expense account.

He went on to study for his MBA, and completed it by the time he was 32; all looked good for John his family and his career.

Then One Day...

John met Helen, an old school friend, in a coffee shop. Helen had left school with no qualifications and had drifted from job to job for a few years since she left school.

When John asked what she was doing now, she replied;

"I live in France now, I have my own consulting business and I love what I do..."

What car do you drive...? asked John...

"What difference does it make...? I fly to most places I need for my business, and I have an office at home too..."

This made John think...

How could Helen, without any qualifications have built her own business that she clearly loved, be living the dream in France and be master of her own destiny...

How could she not care about the car she drove - he loved his A6, it gave him status and authority and it looked good in the golf club car park.

Over time this got John to thinking - he should start his own business. He had the experience, the MBA and the contacts, he should really go out on his own...

As time went on he found that he didn't enjoy his job anymore, the conversation with Helen resounded inside his head and grew ever louder; his dissatisfaction grew each month until...

So he decided to start his own business...

Being an MBA, he looked at the Niche, the Market, the Investment and the projected cash flow forecast for the first five years based on Sales and Margin targets...

He looked at the Marketing to include Web, Social Media and Direct Sales, he even priced up offices and lease cars so that he would be sure he had covered everything.

The plan looked good, so he shared it with his wife and a few close friends; he didn't get the response he anticipated...

What if you don't make Sales...?

What if you don't get the Clients...?

You have a mortgage and children, it is too risky; wait until later...

John worked out that if he didn't achieve his plan he would run out of money and lose the house, car and everything. No more Audi A6, 32 days holiday, fancy house and expense account...

Suddenly John's job looked more attractive, safe and secure; he decided to wait until the mortgage was paid, until the children left home and until he was sure he could make it work...

Some years later, John met Helen in the same Coffee shop and decided to ask her advice.

"If there was one tip that you could give me about starting my own business, what would it be...?"

Helen replied...

"Simple, be prepared to **risk everything you have in order to achieve what you want**, if you are not prepared to lose them, they will simply remain a millstone round your neck that prevents you from achieving anything..."

John thought about what she said. It was an overwhelming FEAR of losing what he had that was preventing him going for what he wanted. The risk of losing his house, car, expense account and lifestyle was simply too great; it became his single debilitating focus that meant he traded Unhappiness for Fear and stayed where he was; employed...

He had become dependent upon his lifestyle, and that which we are dependent upon controls us; so he chose to do nothing...

Epilogue...

By the time John was 45, the company he worked for was sold and his job made redundant. All the things that made him feel safe and comfortable were taken away from him at the stroke of a pen; his Fears became his reality...

As he sat in the Coffee shop bemoaning his fate, he saw Helen; she wandered over and asked how he was doing, he explained what had happened...

"I wish that I had taken the risk years ago, now it is too late and I am too old to start a business; I have lost my job, car and status..."

"Perfect..." said Helen...

"What do you mean...?"

"Now you have nothing to lose, you have nothing to risk and there is no Fear - this is the perfect time for you to start your business..."

John thought about what she said, but decided to look for a Job with an Audi A6, 32 Days holiday and an expense account; he missed the warm comfort of his familiar millstone...

And the moral to the tale of **How to Succeed in Business**...

Risk everything you Have in order to achieve what you Want.

Don't let the thin veneer of Material Wealth conspire against your Happiness.

What you own can be Taken from you if you don't Control what produces it.

You Don't have as much Time as you think.

You can make either Results or Excuses - *but not both*.

The 7 Mistakes that 82% of start-ups make

April 13th, 2014

...Number 3 May Really Surprise You...

These mistakes apply to Start Ups and even those companies who have made it past the critical Two and Five Year point...

As a Business Coach, I get contacted by all sorts of people in business, and if I had to boil them down the most common mistakes that they make to just Seven, these would definitely make it onto the list...

1. **Lack of Cash #1** - starting a business without enough cash to support the investment that is required to hit break even, and begin to achieve positive cash flow...

    This usually comes from over ambitious assumptions being made with regard to the time required to get clients, coupled with an under estimate of the cash required to cover the costs.

    To most Start Ups; assume it will take twice as long as you anticipate, and cost twice what you had budgeted - if you can cover that you will may be OK...

2. **Lack of Cash #2** - once a business has got established, and overcome the initial cash challenges, it will usually hit another one in order to maintain growth.

    As sales activity increases and new clients are attracted-especially in the B2B sectors - cash will be drained from the

---

business quicker than margin can be made; major culprits include;

Discounting to win larger contracts - stop doing this...

Fixed costs increasing in steps - Gross margin may be OK but your Net sucks...

Debtor Days increase while Creditor Days decrease - avoid this too...

Increased stock, WIP, Finished goods and SDNI hold up cash...

Remember, fast growth is that quickest way to kill a business - no business goes bust for lack of Sales, it is usually lack of Cash that does the trick...

3. **Excess Cash** - *sounds ridiculous but...*

In the USA I was approached at an event by someone who had just decided to start his own consultancy business. He told me that he had $75,000 in savings and wanted to know what I thought he should do to get started quickly...

I asked him what his monthly fixed costs were, including marketing and overheads; they were around $10,000 per month...

So I said that in my opinion, he should put $20,000 into the business, and the other $55,000 into a secure account that he could not easily access; this would focus him on getting the business moving quickly rather than living on his savings.

If he had to get clients before the money ran out, then he would; needs must.

He could do this after $20,000 or $75,000 - *the choice was his.*

He didn't like this advice, and it was around 8 months later I had a call from him. He explained that he lived off his $75,000 and when it was gone he signed his first client; and that if he had tucked the $55,000 away, he would have signed clients earlier and kept the money too - and expensive lesson in how too much cash can slow people down...

4. **Hope as a Strategy** - the misguided hope that because a product or service is good; it will attract clients to buy.

Having a passion for the product or service is not enough; you will have to be a Sales and Marketing expert too, or at least find someone who can do this for you.

Customers don't buy what you sell; they buy the consequences of what you sell when they are derived as benefits to them. No one wants to hire an Accountant, Lawyer or Business Coach; they want the results or outcomes that can be derived as a consequence.

If your marketing says **WHAT** you do and ignores the **BENEFITS** that can be expected, there is a huge opportunity being missed...

5. **Vision & Purpose** - going into business with the sole purpose of making money will fail.

    I see lots of people who start, or invest in a business with the sole purpose of getting rich; and whilst of course we are in business to make money, it should not be the only focus.

    Clarity of Vision, Mission and Purpose are critical - what difference do you want to make in the world, how much value can you deliver to people...?

    If you provide a product or service with passion and add value in excess of the price ticket, you will make money; but money should not be the primary focus...

    Imagine, a prospect asks you why you are in business and you say...

    "to get rich, but a Ferrari and retire..."

    not as attractive as...

    "we are in the business of delivering happiness..." c/o Zappos, Las Vegas.

I know which company I am more attracted to - Zappos went from start up to being sold for $1.2 Billion in 5 years with this simple mantra...

6. **Bad Recruiting** - your team can be your biggest asset or your biggest liability, it is up to you which they become...

The number of small companies who hire people without knowing what they are doing astounds me. whilst you may hire people on their skills and experience, you will fire 95% of them on their attitude - so hire them this way...

Hire people who buy in to your Vision, Mission and Purpose; hire people with positive attitude over qualifications. Hire people you would be prepared to socialise with; if you wouldn't then neither will you team and clients...

7. **Burnout** - attempting to everything themselves and assuming that they actually know enough to make the business a success; it's exhausting...

Quitting is the biggest destroyer of most businesses; the owners either literally or metaphorically give up and stop fighting to achieve their dream - it simply gets too hard.

The way round this is to do two things;

Keep Learning - read books, watch videos, go to seminars and events. "Worker harder on yourself than yo do on your business..." - Jim Rohn

Get Help - look for the experts to give you advice and guidance. Reaching out is not a sign of weakness, it is a sign of pragmatism and lack of ego which will serve you well.

8. **Enough is Enough** - it is not good enough anymore to simply keep your promises; you have to achieve more with less...

Assuming that what worked last week will work this week, or that "satisfied" customers are the objective simply won't cut it in today's market place.

Building a client base of raving fans is the best way to sustain your business on the basis of your reputation; always be innovating and looking for ways to over deliver.

We are in the Social Media age, having positive stories out there based upon what you and your team did that was "amazing" will do more for your bottom line than any advert ever can...

Take the Banana Box Challenge

April 30th, 2014

Since we were married in 1986, Lynn and I have had 13 homes in 3 countries on 2 continents, and each time we move, we know that packing delicate articles requires specialist packing in trusty Banana Boxes...

These boxes are generally made of Double Wall Corrugated Cardboard as opposed to the Single Wall material used in Apple or even Orange boxes; they stack really well, are ventilated and have an opening in the lid so that the contents can be seen without removing it...

Trust me on the Banana Boxes...

A couple of weeks ago, a friend in Germany told me that his Grandfather had died at the ripe old age of 92, and the task of clearing his house and looking after all the "arrangements" had fallen to him...

The one thing that affected him the most, apart from the obvious grief at the loss of a member of the family; *was what was actually left behind.*

He showed me into his garage, where stacked up at the back, were around a dozen Banana Boxes containing papers, trinkets and the remaining evidence of a life.

He looked at them and simply said;

"It is really sobering to think that after 92 years, a life gets compressed into just a few boxes at the back of a garage..."

In the boxes were catalogues, brochures and pictures; there was also a number of "To Do" lists, invitations to parties and events that had remained unopened.

There was a blank passport application form, and numerous Post It notes attached to pages of magazines and flyers.

It seemed as if it was a collection of missed opportunities, where "thinking about it" had replaced "Let's do it..."

One Day...

One day, when you have completed your life, someone will be looking at a similar set of your Banana Boxes at the back of a garage; the contents of which may be the only physical reminder of who you were and what you did...

Your Banana Box Challenge - **BBC** - is simply this;

What will be in the boxes you leave behind...?

Will they be filled with memories of a life fully lived, or evidence of procrastination? Will they be filled with joy, amusement and fulfilment or fear, worry and regret...?

What would your **BBC** look like right now - is there space for more achievement, fun, contribution and travel...?

The time to start filling your **BBC** is now - we all have less time than we think, so how about if right now you made the one decision that you have been putting off, made the call you have been avoiding or simply said yes to the opportunity that you have been denying...

When strangers and family look through your Banana Boxes neatly stacked at the back of some garage; what will they find...?

The Career Curveball Paradox

May 1st, 2014

Being Fired was a defining moment...

By the age of 30 I had been trained as a Weapons Engineer and spent 6 years building my career in the Military Subcontracting, Logistics and Supply Chain sector - I had been the youngest Supervisor and Manager in the company and had recently been "head hunted" by a competitor to be their youngest Operations Manager...

Life was good, I was confident, ambitious and effective; my career was on track, with a great salary and a golden opportunity to get a seat on the Board within a couple of years...

So it came as somewhat of a surprise, after just 10 months to be sat down by the Chairman and simply "invited to resign"; it appeared that making changes had ruffled the feathers of the other Managers and they didn't like it - I had made them look bad...

This meant that of the two big players in the Industry, I had resigned from one and been fired by the other - *my options were somewhat limited...*

Ouch...!

I remember going home and lying on the bed staring at the ceiling wondering if my "glittering" career was over, if I would ever find a job again or if I would end up flipping Burgers...

Looking back and joining the dots - this #careercurveballs was actually a defining moment that enabled (*or forced...*) me to make changes in my career that would propel me towards achieving the business and lifestyle of my dreams.

That feeling of negativity, anger and fear actually drove me on to find opportunities that otherwise I would have missed. Most people in my experience wait round for their "Old Job" to simply reappear somewhere else, and of course it rarely does...

From Guns to Dresses and Planes...

I chose to reinvent myself and my career - from Weapons Engineering I went to work at the Worlds No1 Ballroom Dancing Dress making company (*slight change of path...*) then ran Heathrow, Gatwick and Stansted Airports for an Aviation Business.

With my wife, Lynn, we started a Recruitment Agency and formed our Business Coaching and Training Company 12 years ago.

We have lived and worked in the UK and the USA - *based out of Las Vegas* - and have achieved life and business goals that would not have been possible had I not been fired...

We now live in France and travel the World working with Entrepreneurs, Executives and Business Owners - we are fortunate to be able to do what we love with people we like...

Being fired was the best thing that happened to me - it didn't feel like it at the time, but with the benefit of 20:20 hindsight, it was the darkest of days that simply allowed a new dawn to break...

My learning from that experience is that even when Life and Business throws you a curveball, it's not the end but the opportunity for a new beginning - but you have to be prepared to change and embrace the new path, hoping that your old job or career will somehow resurrect itself is in my view a waste of precious time...

When life throws you a Curveball - *which it will* - treat it as an opportunity to change rather than an excuse to withdraw...

Sell anything to anyone if…

May 12th, 2014

...how a Donkey could have changed history...

On the 22nd August 1485 During the battle of Bosworth when his horse, Surrey, is killed and he is unable to escape, find more troops, or indeed be seen by his existing troops, Richard III feared that all would be lost.

In his frustration, Richard knows that the most valuable thing in the world to him at that moment is a horse.

"A horse, a horse, my kingdom for a horse..."

Shakespeare quotes Richard as saying as he knows that all is potentially lost and at that precise moment he recognises that if he doesn't find a horse he will lose his kingdom and therefore the horse was of equal value to him at that moment...

As it happens, no horse becomes available and Richards III is killed and the victorious Henry Tudor, Earl of Richmond was crowned King Henry VII and effectively brought to an end the Plantagenet Dynasty making it a defining moment in both English and Welsh history.

So...

How different could it have been if Richard could have had a horse...?

Now I want you to imagine yourself as a Horse Seller...

To be precise I want you to imagine that on the 21st August during the preparations for the battle you attempt to sell Richard III a new horse - *to replace Surrey, his trusted steed...*

The answer you would have got would have been NO...

Now imagine that if you could make the same offer, for the same Horse to Richard at the precise moment on the following day just after Surrey is tragically killed and he realises that all is potentially lost...

The answer you would of got would have been a resounding YES and the price would have been considerably higher too...

Timing is everything...

In Sales it is not that people don't need your product or service, it is just that they don't need it at the precise time you offer it to them...

You have been told that defining your Target Market and pitching Benefits rather than Features is the way to close a deal. On the day before the Battle your horse could have been faster, stronger and able to jump higher than any other horse; but it wouldn't have been enough to convince Richard III to change Surrey...

24 hrs later however, a scabby donkey with mange and a weak pulse would have been qualification enough to close yourself a very nice deal - *all that changed was the time of the offer...*

When timing is with you, your price increases and your quality

reduces; not that you need to deliver inferior products, but if a donkey would do, sell 'em that, not a thoroughbred.

So defining a target is one thing but choosing your time is critical; it is only "NO now", not "NO forever"...

Keep in touch with your prospects, your offer doesn't need to change, their circumstances will and that may be enough to give you the edge. Remember, when the need arises they will buy from whom ever springs to mind; make sure that it is you they think of first...

One Day things will be different

May 14th, 2014

...One day,1hr 57 minutes will feel like a lifetime...

One day you will give anything to have just one more day...

One Day, people in white coats will shake their head before they give you the news, they will start the sentence with "I'm sorry..." and tell you that it's all coming to an end...

People will stand around and look at you through water logged eyes and wish that they'd had more time to play with their Dad or more time to talk to their Mum; and they will wonder why you spent all your time working so hard you missed them growing up...

Someone will get a 'phone call telling them that if they want to say good bye to you, they need to get to the hospital quick; they will drive across countries to get there and miss you by 1hr 57 minutes...

You will trade all that you have just to walk on grass, to hold her hand again just once more or tell him that you loved him, forgive him and that he's your best friend...

You will wish you had finished early and gone to the beach, learnt Spanish, played the Drums or taken up Salsa...

You'll wish that you hadn't been so angry and quick tempered, you'll wish that you could take it back and undo the tears that you caused...

You won't think about your Car, the Rolex the Gucci and Chanel; when your life flashes before you it will be the people not the brands, your relationships not your acquisitions that shine the brightest - *and you'll wonder why you wasted some much time on them...*

One day you'll remember that you never said, "I love you..." enough and didn't walk in the park in the rain at midnight because it's not what grownups do...

You will look at the ceiling and pray to your new-found God that you should be given more time, you'll beg for, and trade all that you have for a few precious hours to make it all right...

But that day is not Today...

This day is a gift - all the things that you'll beg for and give anything to have more of in your final hours, you have right here and right now...

This day is a good day - you are alive and can walk on grass, hold her hand, tell him you love him and that he's your best friend...

You can travel across countries just to say hi and being 1hr 57 minutes late won't make a difference...

Today you can go to the beach, start learning Spanish, play the Drums and begin to Salsa.

Right now, you can be kinder to yourself and everyone around you, choose to love and be happy...

This day you can realise it's the *people* that matter most and not what you pay for but what is given for free - you can pick up the 'phone and tell them what they should hear...

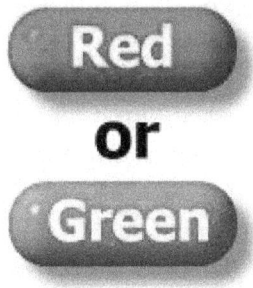

So what will you do with this day that has been gifted - will this be the day that you decide to be different...?

Is this the day that you will thank your future self for when the people in white coats come to you with the news...?

This could be your Matrix moment - question is which one will you choose...?

One Day is Today - *make it count...*

Epilogue - why 1 hr 57 Minutes counts...

In August 2010, I had the 'phone call that if I wanted to say goodbye to my Dad I had better get to the hospital...

I was in Barcelona, he was in Shropshire in the UK and with no flights, the quickest way was to drive - so I drove through the night like a maniac through Spain and France back the UK...

It is 1750 km from Barcelona to Shropshire and takes 16 1/2 hours to drive...

En route I got a 'phone call telling me that he had gone and that I had missed him. I checked the GPS and I was just 1 hour and 57 minutes away...

In 80 years of his life, I missed him by the most important 1 hr and 57 minutes of it, and I have never forgiven myself...

So now when I do events - I make them 1 hr and 57 minutes long - *because I know that that length of time can change a life...*

Get a Job, Retire and Die

May28th 2014

...Tupperware; and Spoons for Drumsticks...

Do you remember being at School and being given "Careers Advice" by a uninterested middle aged underachiever...?

I do, I was told I had two choices; either go down the Pit or join the Army.

Both looked like sensible options until I had the "dream" that I should really aspire to achieve explained to me. Apparently, I should get qualified, find a job (packaged as a "career" to make it sound attractive...) take out a huge loan to buy a house, save any spare cash into a pension - *then retire and die 50 years later.*

I didn't want a "career" at 13 years old I wanted to be a Drummer; specifically, I wanted to be the drummer in The Jam, Rick Buckler was not one of the "greats" and I knew I could do better.

I can remember playing drums on my Mum's Tupperware using spoons for drumsticks and thinking that a normal career would not suit me very well...

But I was told that I would never make any money as a Drummer, and that in order to get a "good job" I should concentrate on getting qualifications and a trade that "no-one could take off me..."

Oh yes and get married and have 2.4 children in the process...

Live the Dream...

We have all been sold the same dream. Generation Y and Millennial's, have it even worse now than us Generation X's did...

Now you have to have a degree to flip a burger, if you want any job that involves a desk then you need a Masters - there are more people in low level admin jobs with MBA's than there are in the Boardroom; academic inflation is the curse of the young...

I see people in jobs they don't like, but because it pays well and supports the Mortgage (translated as; contract until death...) they put up with the politics, boredom, and routine that eventually defines them.

One of my friends has been in the same job since she left school - she is 43 now and has been there for 25 years. The company has been sold and she is being made redundant; her world has fallen apart because the dream she was sold was not true.

What to Do...

I thank that career advisor every day, she was the one that put fear and loathing into my mind as a teenager. She empowered me to do things differently; it didn't feel like it at the time, but her advice was the best I was ever given, she showed me what I didn't want and forced me to explore what I did...

Simply put - you have to let go...

Let go of the house, the car the salary and the status - it is the scariest thing in the world and also the most rewarding. Choose you dream and live it, stop waiting for the "right time" or the best opportunity, or the redundancy cheque or when the kids grow up.

There is a CEO in the UK who meets with me occasionally. He tells me that he is very entrepreneurial and has the right skills and attitude to be a Business Owner.

Last time we met, he pulled up in his silver Audi A6, wearing his Hugo Boss suit, silk tie and Rolex watch. I rolled up on my motorbike in leathers with full face helmet, Kevlar jeans and boots...

Over lunch he told me all about how great he was, and how unhappy it was making him. He told me that when the "time was right" he was going to resign and go out on his own, he just needed a bit more money and time to plan...

He asked my advice - I said leave the car here, text your resignation, go home and get on with it...

To him this was most amusing, but I was serious; he clearly was not...

Three times in my "career" I have sold or left everything and started a new venture. Including moving abroad twice and changing career numerous times...

He is drowning in his Career, his material acquisitions and financial instruments are dragging him down - he needs to let go, but he can't. The **FEAR** of loss is greater than his need for **FREEDOM**...

The only instrument I need is a Drum Kit, and the only FEAR I have is that we don't move fast enough...

I am still married to Lynn, the girl I met at High School, we have two amazing sons and our lives continue to rock. So remember, don't let go of everything, just the things that are holding you down..

At 22 I had no Idea

May 30th, 2014

When I was 22 I had just completed my Mechanical and Production Engineering Apprenticeship at Royal Ordnance Enfield - specialising in Assault Weapons, Sniper Rifles and Cannon up to 30mm calibre...'

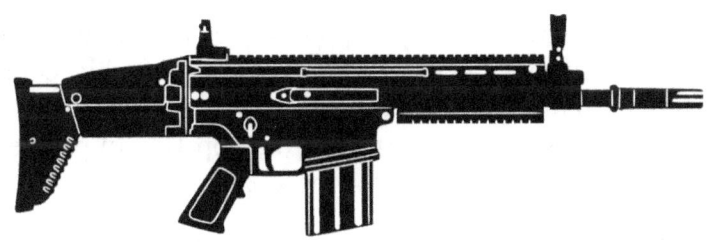

In the previous 5 years I had left home, slept in railway stations, eaten at charity shelters and been on numerous Police Identity Parades - somehow, I had qualified with the Best Overall Technician Apprentice Award, an HNC in Engineering and landed a job as a Professional & Technology Officer...

I remember sitting in the cafe at Euston station waiting for the 18.10 to Birmingham and wondering where I would be when I was 40 or even 50. I imagined my future self, wandering into the cafe and sitting opposite to me and telling me what the future held...

Well, now I am 50 and **#IfIWere22** this is the advice I would give if I could walk into that cafe...

1. **You are going to be OK** - life has a habit of doing a better job of looking after us than we know, trust your instincts and dream more than worry. Worrying is simply praying for what you don't want.

2. **Qualifications Suck** - work on your attitude and passion rather than your Masters and PhD. You are not here to have a stable corporate career until someone decides they want to downsize you at 50; you are here to make a difference, have fun and play nice.

3. **Say Yes and Show Up** - opportunities will come to you. They may come dressed in blue overalls not white collars, but when they do Say Yes to them, Show Up and do your best. Saying yes will put you in the Top 10% of people and Showing Up puts you in the top 2%.

4. **It's not the Money** - money is simply the barometer by which you can measure the value you add to others. If you want more money, add more value, make a bigger difference, make a better contribution. Don't make money your single focus, a life built on greed makes you money rich, but life poor.

5. **Love** - go on the journey with someone, it can get rough out there and having a mate with you helps it all make sense. Find your soul mate, tell them you love them hold their hand every day, stand up for them, lie down with them; sing, laugh and dance the Tango at midnight.

6. **Planning Sucks too** - if you want to give your God a good laugh, tell her your Plans. No one has any idea where they will be in the next 5 years let alone 10 or 20. The job you will be doing in 10 years hasn't been invented yet, your job

is to keep learning, stay open and be prepared to change when needed.

7. **No One Knows** - in reality, no one knows what they are doing, everyone is living on either hope or fear and masking over them with a Gucci Suit, Breitling Watch and a BMW. Get good at being uncertain and don't get too comfortable. "If everything feels under control, you are not going fast enough" - Mario Andretti

Would I want to know then what I know now...?

No - the joy of life is not the knowing it's the discovering. Since I was 22 I have been married to my best mate, Lynn, for 28 years, we have two amazing sons, we've lived in 10 homes in the UK, two in Las Vegas and two here in France.

Our lives have taken twists and turns that have made us fortunes and lost us a few too, we have great friends an amazing business and we are not done yet...

We are in the second half of the game and we are winning 5-3...

Are we where we thought we'd be...?

Nowhere near - *thank goodness* - the problem is that at 22 we can only make plans based on what we know is possible at that time; we don't realise it but our ambitions are probably our biggest limiting factors.

In that station cafe, I simply hoped to be able to find a job, get a house and pay a mortgage; I had no clue that I would end up living in Las Vegas and then in what was the Italian Ambassadors previous home on the Moselle Valley.

If I had the privilege of offering advice to another 22-year-old about to launch their career, I would simply guide them to follow their Dreams, trust their Heart and enjoy the ride.

Why the Rich Don't Retire

June 1st, 2014

...what would they retire from...?

In a 2013 study in the USA it was found that when asked "At what age do you plan to retire...?" around One Third of people with annual earnings of over $750,000 said "over 70" with 15% saying "never..."

Only 6% of those making under $100,000 plan to retire at 70, most planned to retire by 65.

Globally, 60% of those with a net worth of $15 million or more will continue to work "no matter what their age..."

Meanwhile in France...

In 2010 members of the Public and Private sectors a series of General Strikes and Demonstrations were held throughout September and October. They involved union members from both the public and private sectors protesting in Bordeaux, Lille, Paris, Marseilles and Strasbourg.

The strikes led to a national fuel shortage, reduction in public transport services and students barricading 400 high schools to prevent them from opening...

The excuse for this action - raising the statutory age of retirement from 65 to 67...

So why the paradox of the rich retiring later than the poorer...?

Simple - *because it's not about the money...*

It's about mindset; when you love what you do, why would you retire from it...?

There is a reason a salary is called "compensation" - it is compensating someone for the time they expend in the job they do, and also for taking the fun and enjoyment out of 2000 hours a year they have to be "at work..."

When people don't enjoy what they do - of course they want to retire. They will want more holiday and sickness cover as well - anything to get time away from the job...

Not all jobs are like this of course but in another study only 13% of employees said that they were "engaged and enjoying..." their work. The rest were disengaged at best with 24% "hating..." their work...

Not really that surprising that employees want to retire...

Business Owners, Entrepreneurs and Solopreneurs don't want to retire - it's just too much fun...

Now, for all those business owners who groaned at my use of the "F.." word, if it wasn't fun on balance you wouldn't do it...

Can you imagine the Queen of England moaning about retirement age, or Keith Richards wanting to join the Ramblers Association...?

Has Jack Welch stopped working, is Richard Branson looking to potter around and play crown green bowls...?

Do you think that David Bowie who was born in 1947 - ever phones in sick on a Monday, or turn his 'phone off on a Sunday...?

Is Warren Buffet, who was born in 1930, protesting about or worrying about the statutory retirement age, or his holiday and sickness entitlement...?

Of course, not...

People may look at them and say, "it's OK for them, they are rich and they enjoy what they do..."

In reality of course, it is the other way round. They have a passion and talent for what they do, and the riches have come to them because of that; being rich is a by-product of passion driven activity.

It is possible of course to be employed, happy and not retire. Take the case of Morris Miller in the USA who at age 100 is still working for McDonald's; he has been there for 25 years and didn't start until he was 75...!

The formula for being rich, and not wanting to retire - which includes Life Rich, Family Rich, Time Rich and Money Rich is;

(Passion x Talent) + Time = Wealth

Where Passion and Talent are the main drivers, and time is secondary. If you want more Wealth, get more Passionate about your Talent...

The formula for being poor and hoping for retirement including Life Poor, Family Poor, Time Poor and Money Poor is;

Time x Work = Wage

Where the only way to get more Wage is to work longer and harder, time is primary...

If you want more money, do overtime and work weekends...

If you are looking forward to holidays, calling in sick on a Monday and protesting about the retirement age, you haven't found your passion or exercised your talent yet.

The Rich don't retire because they can't, they are what they do. Work Life Balance does not compute; they are one and the same. Retiring from one means retiring from the other.

The quickest way to cure 94% of all known illnesses, colds, flu and headaches is to own your own business...

Find your talent, release your passion and follow your dream. If you can do that within your job like Morris Miller then good for you, make it your life's work and it becomes play, and playtime should never end...

Life Lessons from Troy Tempest

June 4th, 2014

...stand by for Action...

For Beatrice...

This Blog is dedicated a lady called Beatrice, whom I have never met or spoken with, but heard a little bit about. When I was told that she was "thinking" about starting her own business - I wondered if I could give her a bit of gentle guidance...

When I was a child - one of my favourite TV programs was Stingray...

Filmed in VideoColor & SuperMarionation, and remembered by a few of the early Generation X readers here, it had all the advice we needed to get ahead and be successful...

The Top Success Tips from Troy Tempest & Stingray;

1. Stand by For Action - not wait around until the time is right for Action...

2. Anything can happen in the next 1/2 hour - be prepared for the unexpected...

3. Good Guys finish first - Troy, Phones and Marina always won...

4. Love Rules OK - in each show Marina and Troy get cosy on a beach...

So why do so many people not heed these lessons...?

There is a medical condition that affects the majority of people, it is called Contingent Action Hypoactivity Syndrome - or **CAHS** for short...

The condition was extensively studied at the University of Prague during the 2004 under the guidance of Professor Otálení Na Hovno and his team.

The study found that given a set of opportunities or decisions to make, 84.3% of people choose to say no and do nothing.

Another 7.7% of people may make a positive choice to change, but delay taking action until they feel the conditions are better.

And only 8% of people actually say yes, and take immediate action towards the achievement of the opportunity that has been presented to them...

In other words - 92% of the population were suffering from CAHS; the inability to either make a decision at all, deciding to take action and delaying the start point indefinitely. The study found that Fear, Worry, Uncertainty and lack of Confidence were the key drivers of the behaviour.

Relax, a Cure is available...

In his landmark publication "Scared of the D.A.R.K..." Author and Business Coach David Holland, built on the work of Professor Na Hovno and defined a model for achievement that, to date, has been the only cure for severe cases of CAHS...

It is suggested by Holland that most people approach business and life in a structured way.

1. **Knowledge** - first they get qualified.

2. **Resources** - then they attempt to accumulate resources.

3. **Action** - they get busy with life and career.

4. **Dream** - when it's too late they realise they didn't live the Dream.

This fits well into the original research and serves to define further the symptoms of CAHS...

Furthermore, Holland suggests that the 8% of people who are unaffected by the CAHS syndrome display a significantly different sequence to the same symptoms;

1. **Dream** - they start with a Vision for themselves...

2. **Action** - they take action quickly...

3. **Resources** - trusting they will show up when needed...

4. **Knowledge** - learning as they go they take risks of failure...

So, if you find yourself suffering from a debilitating case of CAHS - simply refer to the **D.A.R.K** system, and Beatrice; remember not to be scared of it...

How to make your Business Grow

June 8th, 2014

In this Blog you'll find the answer to the question "How to make my business grow...?"

Whether you're a Start Up or Established there is a simple rule that applies to achieving growth;

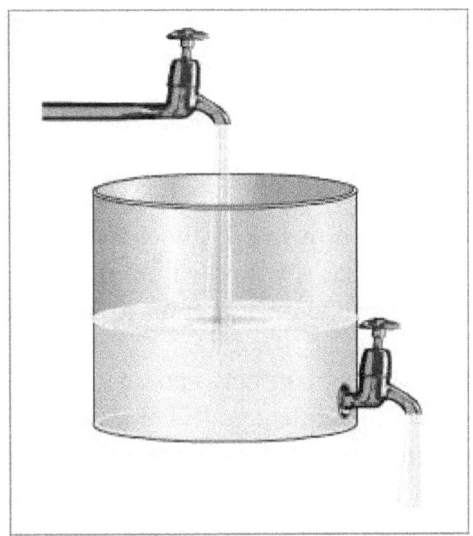

It is called the Principle of **Dynamic Equilibrium**, and once your business achieves it, growth will stop; *so our challenge is how to avoid it...*

Simply put, when your business loses customers at the same rate as it gains new ones, you are in Dynamic Equilibrium.

Put it another way, the bucket is leaking as fast as you can fill it...!

So, the first step in getting your business back in to growth is to figure out where the opportunity for improvement lies.

Do we need to fix the leak, or do we need a bigger hose...?

Fixing the Leak...

This is the cheapest and easiest place to start, in fact way too many businesses waste huge amounts of time and money on Marketing and Sales, simple because they don't fix the leak first...

What to measure depends on your business, here are some examples...

Martial Arts Business - how many students are you losing each month, in other words what is your attrition rate. If it is over 5% then it's worth spending time on strategies to improve here first.

Retail Business - how long is it between visits from your customers. The dwell or frequency of visit is a key driver of success here. First measure what the numbers are and then look for ways to increase the pace of activity with all customers.

Consulting Business - how long do clients stay with you for...? In business Coaching for example, if your clients are leaving you after 3 months, then there is a huge opportunity for improvement.

What is your innovation program; are you offering obsolete services and products...

When was the last time you surveyed you customers to find out what they think you could improve...?

How good is your Customer Service...?

Try asking your customers "The Ultimate Question" from the excellent book of the same name by Fred Riechheld, and set a target for your future scores as a Key Performance Indicator of your business.

This approach has the added benefit of keeping your customers coming back, and encouraging them to refer new ones to you; a great way of destroying Dynamic Equilibrium...

Getting a Bigger Hose...

If your Attrition, Retention and Dwell are all under control, then another way (apart from going down the acquisition route...) to grow your business is to attract more customers.

Beware, Marketing and Sales is very inefficient; what I mean is that not all that you do will work, in fact most of what you do may not generate any direct response at all and remember, it's a process not an event...

First, lets be clear on what Marketing and Sales actually are...

Marketing - gets the 'phone to ring, or an enquiry to be made. It may get people in room with you or to attend a meeting. It is simply designed to get Leads...

There are two types of marketing; Above the Line and Below the Line. Basically, ABL is general non-targeted activity, whilst BTL is targeted and directed at a specific niche or sector.

You will need to do both, but the more BTL strategies you have, the better. Remember in the SME sector we do not have a Brand to promote. We simply have a message and a reputation that we need to get to our target audience, such that they feel compelled to make contact...

Sales - is the process of converting the leads generated from your marketing activity into paying customers. This is the "funnel" or "pinch point" through which all your prospects must pass, and is where, in my experience, there are huge improvements to be made in lots of businesses.

There are plenty of people who are great at what they do. They get Leads from their Marketing team via SEO, Telemarketing or Seminar Invites, but when it comes to converting them to customers it all falls apart...

The conversion rate defines the success of your Marketing and Sales activity.

Leads x Conversion % = # Customers

Being a great Accountant, Martial Artist, Web Designer or Recruiter is simply not enough, the process of conversion has to be based on Value and Benefits, not Price and Attributes.

Getting good at Sales is one of the most effective ways there is to grow your business and maximise the growth potential you have...

Finally, they key to answering the question "how do I grow my business...?" is to understand the factors that are affecting it; don't simply throw money at Marketing if your problem is Customer Service. Don't offer discounts if the problem is Sales and conversion ability.

In fact - *don't offer discounts ever...*

The trick is to identify what is actually preventing your business from achieving growth, and acting accordingly...

Should you be Making Waves...?

June 29th, 2014

...as you transmit; so shall you receive...

Imagine that you are kneeling next to a bath tub filled around half full of water...

Place your hand into the water and move it from left to right...

If you move your hand quickly, you cause ripples and splashes- its hard work and soon gets tiring, all you cause is a disturbance in the water...

There is a speed of hand movement, however, that will have the water swooshing to the back and then to the front of the bath in a big wave - still only based on the movement of your hand. This is when the pace, or frequency of movement, of your hand is in resonance with the water in the bath; you are in resonance with the system...

At this frequency of movement, and being in resonance, you will feel comfortable and in control, in fact if you stop pushing, the water will keep momentum and push you back...

When a system is in resonance, it will tend to oscillate (vibrate...) at a greater amplitude (bigger movements...) at a given frequency of input...

People too are both transmitters and receivers of Vibrational energy from the world, people and "systems" around us...

What we choose to resonate, or be in harmony with, is a choice we have and a strategy we can use for achievement, success and happiness...

Negative Vibes...

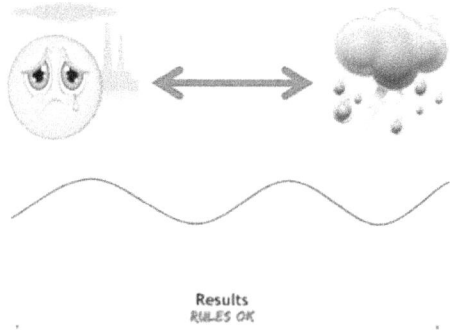

Results
RULES OK

Imagine someone is displaying or transmitting low frequency or negative energy - they will resonate with other low or negative energies. They will feel comfortable with other people, situations and opportunities whose "systems" resonate at that frequency...

They will attract these people, situations and opportunities to themselves, because as with the water in the bath, the frequencies they transmit they are in harmony with them, they feel comfortable there; and by definition, different frequencies simply don't feel as "comfortable" or attractive, so they are avoided...

Positive Vibes...

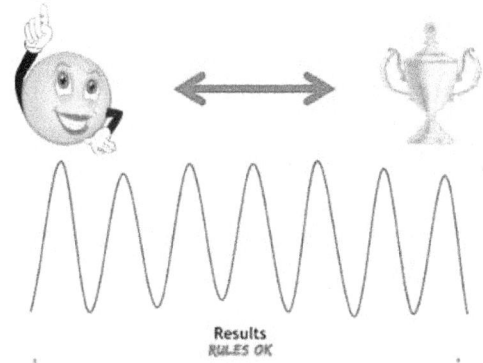

Results
RULES OK

The same applies to those people transmitting high
oe positive energy; they will resonate with other high or positive
energies. They will attract and feel comfortable as they are in
harmony with these different frequencies; they too will attract
similar people, situations and opportunities.

In fact, whatever frequency of vibration you are transmitting -
anything that is not in resonance with your will feel uncomfortable;
we all have people that we somehow don't "resonate" with - of
course you don't you're on a different frequency...

How to take control...

First - check your own levels of energy. Are you truly a positive
person who looks for the good in people and situations...?

Are you honest, open, kind and of high integrity - do you use
positive thoughts, phrases and words in your communication...?

Look at what you are currently attracting - the people, situations and opportunities you attract now are a direct consequence of what you are transmitting...

If you want to improve them - improve yourself. Make yourself attractive and resonant with higher levels of energy and you will by consequence attract the same to you.

Second - once you have got your vibrational energy where you need it to be, check for people around you that disturb your harmony. They are on a different frequency to you and, whilst you should respect them for where they are; move away from them or let them go; you need to create space for others...

People of lower vibrational energy are toxic to your happiness and success, do not let them in; as soon as you raise your energy, they will feel the shift and probably leave you alone anyway...

Third - when people, situations and opportunities arise that you feel comfortable with, are in harmony with your vibrational energy; be prepared to take the risk of saying yes, taking the risk of changing and achieving more...

Success doesn't come when you think about it; it comes when you recognise and accept the opportunity that will enable you to achieve it...

Making waves is a very good idea; *but only if they are Positive...*

Too Ugly to Be Successful...?

July 4th, 2014+

...for anyone who wants to attract new Clients...

Let's just be clear - I don't mean ugly to look at...

There is a clear rule in Sales that you have to be "Attractive" - not physically; but represent an

attractive proposition to your prospects such that they see value in what you are offering and will exchange money for the delivery of your promises...

Of course, it always helps if you are clean, reasonably symmetrical and well-presented when you are selling; but relax you really don't need to be a perfect 10 to be successful...

Probably, most of us are selling a Service - an invisible, intangible. The only way prospects and customers can judge before they buy is what others say, and the experience they have at every level of engagement with us - making the intangible tangible through context…

In business you are doing one of two things with regards to new customers and clients;

1. **Attracting** - you are offering and proposing products and services that are attractive to your target audience, and they are continually moving towards your position. They are developing relationships with you and your company that are based on liking, knowing and trusting all that you stand for.

2. **Repelling** - if you are not attracting, then you are repellent; your business looks ugly. Sounds harsh, but the truth is that you are actually persuading people to not buy from you, or go somewhere else and buy instead. Your prospects have no relationship with you other than uncertainty and ambivalence.

Making yourself less Repellent and more Attractive...

What does an Ugly, Repellent company look like and how do they behave...?

Here's the Top 10 Ugly List...

1. Website is out of date and there is no attractive content that defines what problem is being solved, and what benefits can be derived as a consequence of purchasing.

2. Social Media presence is non-existent, or it is just adverts - or pictures of the owner drinking beer. There is no personality to the information that is published, and the activity is sporadic at best.

3. People are not on time for meetings and appointments, deadlines are not met and promises not kept...

4. The telephone gets answered badly, and when you visit there is no warm welcome; you are ignored unless they think you may spend money with them.

5. Emails are not responded to, and messages are ignored.

6. The Vision, Mission and Values of the business may be defined if you're lucky, but they are simply kept behind the reception desk signed by the Chairman 30 years ago.

7. The business has to rely on aggressive Marketing and Sales for growth because the levels of referrals and introductions are so low they have to sell hard to maintain profitability.

8. The team are not passionate and enthusiastic about the business; they talk about the business in negative terms socially and morale is generally low.

9. The focus of the business is Money first; rather than the value and experience that is delivered to clients.

10. Management leads by fear rather than vision, and ego drives decisions and strategy rather than informed ideas and knowledge based tactics.

So if you **DON'T** do any of the above you will be instantly more attractive, make more money and live a happier life...

What could be better...?

---

10 Rules of Life you should Break...

July 9th, 2014

.... especially #4 and #9...

Marcus Buckingham and Curt Coffman wrote a great book on business success - "First, Break all the Rules..."

Click on the LINK to have look on Amazon and get a copy for yourself...

The question is - which rules are you going to break...?

Before we get started - of course I don't mean that you should break the Rule of Law; we know whose rules they are and breaking them can lead to rocks being broken in the hot sun...

Who gave you the Rules...?

In life we have a checklist of activities and rules that we are "expected" to accomplish and comply with, they include;

Go to school and get good grades...

Get a trade or professional qualification...

Find a job and work 2,000 hrs. per year for 45 years...

...then die early so you are not a burden...

Live with someone and have 2.1 children...

Buy a house with a humongous Mortgage ...

Have a Smart phone, German car and Swiss watch...

Buy toys and appliances on credit...

Trust Politicians, the Banks and big Corporations...

Comply with rules 1 to 9...

I guarantee that these "rules" are not written down anywhere (depending what flavour of Religion you choose to believe of course...) they are self-imposed, and become a self-managing regulatory system. We all fall for it, and whilst we may moan and complain about all of them, only 1% of people actually choose to rebel against them...

Look what happens every day when people break these unwritten rules...

Children who don't "fit the mold" are given named conditions such as ADHD, GAD and OCD then given drugs to control the "disorder" - Ritalin saw a 300% increase in prescriptions between 1999 and 2010.

Those who aren't academically "qualified" find themselves marginalised and excluded from the workplace - academic inflation has made a Degree compulsory for the majority of even simple administrative functions.

Payday Pig, one of many payday loan companies charge 1737% APR on credit loans, made to people who can't afford to comply with Rule #7 & #8.

Rebels and activists are hunted and prosecuted - think here of Julian Assange, and Edward Snowden; they fought Rule #9.

What heinous crimes did these people commit - simple; they didn't comply with the expectations placed onto them by society. Being different from the norm is a threat to the majority - and the majority, whilst individually applauding the free radicals in society, collectively exclude, intimidate and prosecute them by abdicating control to the Politicians, Banks and Corporates. See Rule #9.

In other words - you can buy a **Green Day** Album and sing along to American Idiot in the shower; but you will still drive your BMW to the Corporate offices that pay your wages like a good worker bee; because the loss of the BMW and status is more painful than actually standing up for what you believe in to achieve what you deserve...

We are all compelled through social, political and economic pressure to comply with these industrial age paradigms so that the capitalist machine keeps whirring away behind its shroud of mountebank democracy.

And yet...

The best results and achievements lie just outside the scope of some of these self-imposed rules - I happen to think that being married for 28 years and having two fabulous sons is a rule that I will keep...

Others I choose not to go along with - #3, #8 & #9 particularly...

When asked what he wanted to be when he grew up, John Lennon replied "Happy..."

That falls outside of the rules - hence he became a legendary singer songwriter. The choice we all have is to be happy - the challenge is that we may need to break some of the rules to get there...

Question is - are you prepared to break the rules to achieve your happiness...?

Are you prepared to take the risk of ambition, promotion and entrepreneurship and live the dream - are you prepared to dream at all...?

If you really want to find out what a Dream looks like - ask a 6-year-old what they want to be when they are big. Probably the same things that you wanted to be when you were 6 but were told you wouldn't make any money at, wouldn't be any good at or that you should get a safe secure job with a good salary...

PS - plenty of people fail, get fired or made redundant doing things they don't enjoy; why not take the same risks but doing something that you do...?

Frustrated Ballerinas, Footballers, Dancers and Rock Stars take note...

So instead we sacrifice our dreams and trade them for a life according to the rules that collectively get imposed upon us...

But what if we didn't - what if we broke these rules and simply started to do what would make us happy. Trust me a BMW and a Credit Card are not the keys to happiness...

Choose your dream, change the Rules and go for it...

10 Rules of Business you should Break...

July 29th, 2014

...especially #1 & #5...

I spent 12 years going to college / night-school and university to learn how to run a business. I have an HNC, DMS and an MBA - *with distinction if you don't mind...*

While the content of the courses was academically interesting and challenging; around 90% of the content was delivered by lecturers who had never actually been in business. Most of them had never had a job outside of academia and simply taught us theory after theory that had been selected from books...

Since then, I have been the CEO of other people's companies, built and run my own and now, as a Business Coach, have the privilege of supporting other likeminded Entrepreneurs and Executives in their quest for achievement.

Along the way I have learned that the Rules of business are not what you think, in fact some of the rules are probably killing your sales and success...

Here are the 10 Rules of Business that you should be breaking...

1. **People buy on Price...**

   No, they don't; unless you let them. People buy on Value, Liking, Knowing and Trusting you and your team. I can hear some saying "ahhh, but my business is special, and price is critical..." Unless you are running Wal-Mart, Tesco or Asda it's not necessarily true...

2. **Under Promise and Over Deliver...**

   Another myth - why would you do this. Simple rule in business, make a promise and keep it consistently. Remember that consistent, reliable excellence will beat occasional brilliance any day...

3. **People are motivated by Money...**

   No, they are not - it's just that people are so bad as a boss and leader they need to be paid a lot to put up with them. People respond to recognition, brightness of future, contribution; money satisfies not motivates...

4. **Shareholders are the most important people in a Co...**

   To the Directors they may be as they are employed by them. The most important people in a Co are the **CUSTOMERS**; shareholders only derive value and returns when the customers do...

5. You need Porsche, Breitling & Gucci to be successful...

I was once told that to be good at sales, I needed a 911; rubbish. People buy people, the more "attractive" you are as a professional and the more value you can deliver, the more successful you will become...

6. Management know what they are doing...

People in suits are not always the experts that they pretend to be - look at Politicians, CEO's and Bankers. Use your instinct, reach out to the next generation and keep learning all the time if you want to stay ahead...

7. You need a Business Plan...

Only when you want money from the Bank; if you have a 50-page plan you won't read it anyway do so don't bother. Get a One Page Plan, build a Vision and Mission then get busy. A plan is only a best guess anyway, and 87% are wrong...

8. Can't start a business without money...

Yes you can - or at least you don't need your own money. Think of crowd funding, friends, family and investors. Remember that **OPIUM** may be the key - Other Peoples Investment Using Money...

9. 10% net Profit is good...

It may be adequate - but don't be limited by these generalised goals. It depends what business you are in, but there is no reason why you can't lead the field in terms of net profitability in your sector...

10. Marketing is expensive...

It is when you don't know what you are doing. Marketing done right delivers a ROI; for every £ or $ you spend on Marketing you should get more back in Profit, if you aren't, then stop doing it, and do something else... #business, #inspiration, #entrepreneurship, #sales.

Break the Rules in order to achieve more...

All You know is Wrong...

July 29th, 2014

Government

Wealth Warning

Everything You

Think You Know

Is Wrong

The Rules have Changed,
You are in Control Now

The language of business is numbers, a business can look good, feel good and even taste good; but unless the numbers are right – you won't have a business, you'll just have a very expensive hobby...

My challenge and opportunity therefore is to make your business numbers as compelling and exciting as the passion you have for every other aspect of your life; so here goes...

Here are my **7 Contradictions** that will help you become truly successful...

Contradiction 1 – Profit is not your Objective.

Your objective is to build your business to achieve what you want. Once you are clear on exactly *why* you are in business, we can make a plan. Now while of course you need to make a profit in your business, profit is simply a barometer that lets you know how you are doing, your focus and attention should be on the *causes* of profit – your objective is to understand what causes profit in your business and manage them so that you can achieve your *why*.

Profit is your Objective when you know why, and how to generate it...

Contradiction 2 – Cash is not King.

Cash will produce approximately nothing while it is sat in your account, it will make you feel good and able to sleep at night, but that is all. Cash should be invested in assets and resources that give you a return. For example, the only reason you should pay a wage is because you get a better return on the investment than leaving it in the bank or trading on the markets. It is how you invest your cash that is King, not how you store it. When your cash actually works for you, you will make sure you collect all that is due on time, every time – it will be really expensive when you don't...

Cash is King when it is invested well...

Contradiction 3 – Growth is not Good.

Plenty of profitable businesses close down because they simply grow too fast, they cannot keep pace with the investment required. Imagine a business with revenues of £5 million in 2009 that grows steadily so it achieves total revenue of £6 million in 2010. That's just a 20% increase; but if in January 2010 the sales were around £420k (about 1/12 of the £5 million), to achieve £6 million during the year, assuming steady growth, the sales in December 2010 would need to be around £600k – compared to January that is a change of 42%, not 20% and even if growth stops there – the business will have a running rate of £600k per month, or £7.2 million a year – growing a massive 71%.. Understanding the *implications* of growth is fundamental to your success – *20% growth = 71% bigger...*

Growth is good, only when it is managed and understood...

Contradiction 4 – Big Contracts are Bad.

I have a rule that in any of my companies, one client should represent no more than 10% of my profits. Winning a big contract looks very attractive, especially when you are going for growth – they can be the worst thing that happens to a business. Watch out for tight margins, extended payment terms, and queries raised on your invoices from eager employees' in their Purchase ledger department. If you do go for a big contract, make sure you keep marketing to find others that will dilute their control over you – don't allow a customer to have more control over your business than your shareholders

Big Contracts are great when they contribute to your business not overwhelm it...

Contradiction 5 – Avoid Discounting.

Never ever discount your prices – and don't be fooled by Manufacturers Recommended Retail Prices either... If you make 50% gross profit on an item, and you offer a discount of 25% you will instantly cut your profits in half on every sale. This means that in order to get a benefit from the offer you have got to sell more than twice the amount you would have done at the full price – sounds like working harder to stand still to me… If you put your prices up by 10% on the same item – you could afford to sell fewer and still make the same profit – there are always choices when it comes to pricing, and maintaining your margins is the art of a successful business.

Pricing is the essence of your success – protect your margins wherever possible…

Contradiction 6 – Overheads are Good.

Very few people build a great business by simply cutting costs. Your overheads are usually made up of the salaries and wages of your team, premises costs and other operational necessities. They are not overheads when they all give you a positive return on your investment – see Contradiction 2. When every team member gives you a positive return, you can hire as many as you like, when you pay rent for a great location that generates business for you, open more branches in similar locations. Every line of overhead should be viewed as an investment from which you need to get a return – your insurance broker should pass you referrals, so should your bank and telephone provider. When every overhead is truly working for your business – overheads are indeed good.

Overheads are bad – only when they are out of control…

Contradiction 7 – Accounts is boring.

I love looking at my accounts – now you may say that I need to get out more, but once we understand our business, we can actually start to enjoy looking at how our business is doing. Your accounts should be regular, monthly for the full management accounts but have daily and weekly numbers prepared that will show you what is happening. Select a range of indicators that will let you know how everything and everyone is performing. Marketing, service and operations should all have measures and performance targets to achieve – that will mean when you look at the accounts you will be pleasantly surprised and not unduly shocked.

Accounts are exciting when they tell you good news...

Release Your Kraken...

July 30th, 2014

...and see what you can achieve...

The most amazing, successful and powerful person in the World is locked up inside you....

You probably know them really well - you have conversations with them, you can visualise them and see them leaping tall buildings, building great relationships and achieving abundant success...

They have the ability to live the lifestyle of your dreams, make money, travel and have fabulous relationships with friends and family...

She appears to you in daydreams and wish lists, he haunts your sleep and challenges your routines; they are the grain of sand in your shoe that irritatingly and constantly remind you that you are worth more and able to do more than you are allowing yourself...

So who is this person...?

It's you - but a better, upgraded, turbocharged refined version of you. It's you, but without the baggage, it's you being the best that you can be; it's you as you know you could be...

Where are they...?

Locked away in a cage of your own making, waiting for you to let them out to play...

The Bars are forged from your beliefs, the lock fabricated from the synthetic rules that you create and choose to live by.

Every time you say no to an opportunity, tolerate abuse or negativity, or find an excuse not to learn; more bars are added to the cage...

Talking yourself out of getting on stage, writing your book, or breaking your routine turns the key even further and makes escape even less likely...

The voice inside your head that tells you that you aren't worthy, not attractive enough, clever enough or old or young enough is the voice of your prison warder compelling you to stay put where you are; safe in your cage...

How to free them - *release your Kraken*...

Simple - remove the bars and unlock the door...

Every time you feel yourself complying with your self-imposed rules of scarcity, reluctance and avoidance, make a different choice...

Take the opportunity, say yes to the new job or business venture; take the risk of being successful, take the risk of not doing what your parents expected of you, and take the risk of letting go of what you have so you can achieve what you deserve...

Every time you abandon one of your old rules, a bar of the cage is removed, the key makes a turn in the lock; the person you can become gets a little closer to freedom...

We build cages not to keep us in, but keep the world out. They are safe, comfortable and predictable, but they don't allow us to grow;

they restrict and restrain us, and the safer we feel, the more comfortable we become - the less fun, excitement and achievement we experience...

We are not on the planet to be safe, secure and comfortable. This is not a rest area, or a home for the bewildered; its a theme park, a vibrant action movie with you as the Star, Director, Producer and Writer.

We are only allowed one visit to this place, we may go on to other places afterwards, and we may have been to other places before; but we are here now, together now and now is the only time we have to really see what we can do when break our rules, open the cage and release our Kraken...

Your Early Morning Wake Up Call...

July 30th, 2014

...to the rest of your life...

It was 02.30 in New London, early by anyone's standards, when Kathy's mobile 'phone rang out from the bedside table.

Reaching over still half asleep, her fingers dipped into the glass of water she kept there reminding her of the tricks played out at sleep over parties as a child - the bathroom instantly became a priority destination for her...

Reaching the 'phone in the darkness, she answered it with a subdued and very tired;

"Hello..."

"Hi, is that Kathy Monroe...?

"Yes - who is this...?"

"Sorry, this is Steven Bradbury from Ancestral File .com over in Los Angeles; I have some exciting news for you..."

"Really, at 02.30 in the morning, couldn't it wait...?"

"We thought you should know, as soon as we found out, we just thought you'd like to know as soon as possible..."

"Know what...?"

"That you are actually Kathy Facultas, not Kathy Monroe..."

"What is this, are you some kind of stalker...?"

"No, really - you are Kathy Facultas. The daughter of Robert and Helen Facultas, members of the original Royal Family of Prussia..."

"What, why are you telling me this now, who are you exactly..."

"You have an inheritance and a title. Your family heritage is one of achievement, excellence and wealth, there are great expectations placed upon you and responsibilities you have - we'd like you to come to a meeting in a few weeks time to sort out all the paperwork - I will email you later today..."

Kathy felt confused, tired and disoriented - the strangers voice so early in the morning was unexpected and somewhat bizarre...

The phone went dead - and immediately the bathroom became of urgent importance now.

Yawning and walking back into the bedroom, Kathy started to think about the telephone call - she looked at her 'phone but the last number to call was from a withheld number...

Had she been dreaming...?

At 34 years of age, living in suburban Essex, working in the Building Supplies company that she joined when she left school - life seemed pretty good. She was married with 5-year-old twins and a home and friends that she liked...

Was she really part of a Royal family - she had been adopted as a baby, so it was just possible that she was who Steven Bradbury said she was...

She climbed into bed and slowly drifted off to sleep...

The alarm went at 06.30 and Kathy woke with a start - a night of broken sleep didn't serve her well..

Up, showered, breakfasted, and youngsters to school, Kathy started her commute to the office - *almost forgetting about the 'phone call she had received...*

Royalty indeed, inheritance, expectations and heritage - and here she was working on reception for 15 years...

As she thought about the 'phone call, and the email she would get and the meeting she would attend - she felt herself physically get a little taller. Her head raised and she felt more confident and self aware - she had always "knew" that she was destined for great things and this just served to validate her point...

As she arrived at work she found that it no longer interested her - being a Royal surely meant that she should be drinking champagne not tea out of a mug.

Over the coming weeks she dressed better, found a new job in the city, booked a fabulous family holiday and bought a new car. She started to mix with high flyers, and was so convinced that she was destined for greatness that within 6 months she had started her own company and within 2 years was drinking champagne in Monaco with her family on their yacht...

Strange thing was that the Email never arrived - in fact Kathy convinced herself that the whole conversation that night was just a dream.

However, simply choosing to acknowledge a different possibility, enabled her to create a different reality...

What Wake Up Call call do you think you should get...?

If you were told you were amazing how differently would you behave...?

Sometimes just having a different perception about what is expected of us can have a dramatic effect on who we are, how we behave and the results we achieve...

Who you are BEING affects what you spend your time DOING and ultimately determines what you experience HAVING...

2 Lessons from Nazis doing the Tango...

August 1st, 2014

...creativity shows up in the strangest of places...

In 1941 Germany was on the receiving end of Allied bombing, land campaigns and resistance sabotage. The second World War was beginning to turn against them.

Whilst it wouldn't be until the August of 1942 that the Russians would start the battle for Stalingrad and begin the long march to Berlin - for the Coca Cola Company, getting the ingredients to manufacture Coke was becoming increasingly difficult.

The Trade Embargo enforced by the Allies meant that supplies of the Syrup needed to make Coke was not available, so the German managers at Coca Cola had to be creative...

What could they make that used only ingredients available in Germany...?

I'm sure cabbage and sausage may have sprung to mind, but finally they decided to use Whey and Pomace - the leftovers from the leftovers...

When it came to naming this new "product" they decided to brainstorm the idea as a team. When instructed to get creative and "fantasize" about the potential name - Joe Knipp, one of the team responded "Fanta..."

And hey presto - Fanta was born...

Fanta is still owned by the Coca Cola Company and is now available globally in 90 flavours.

Lesson #1 - make do with what you have. You don't know what is available until you don't have what you need. Sometimes

if you want to get your team to be really creative - starve them of resources and see what they do when their backs are against the wall...

As a side note - In the USA Fanta is marketed by "The Fanatanas..." - I'm pretty sure that they don't realize where the product originated - I can only imagine what the Coca Cola Managers in 1941 Nazi Germany would have thought...

Interesting to note the differences between 1941 Fanta Marketing in Germany and 2012 Marketing in the USA...

In the late 1940's Europe was being rebuilt - and it fell to the Corona Soft Drinks Co to start introducing new products to an eager UK market...

Not being convinced that Fanta - designed and distributed by their recently vanquished foes across the Channel - would be that popular with people; they did what all good businesses do...

They copied Fanta and called it Tango...

In 1950, Corona introduced Tango and under the current owners - Britvic continues to be the main rival to Fanta in the UK market.

Lesson #2 - let others be the Pioneers - it can be a really expensive position to be in and when it looks like it will work - copy it. We call it Market Research nowadays and while we don't need to breach copyrights and patents; we can learn a lot from those who have gone before us.

So there you have it - two lessons from the Nazis and Fanta...

About Results Rules OK

Results Rules OK was created with a simple and clear 2020 vision;

To enable everyone to enjoy learning, achieving, doing and being more...

This is achieved through the delivery of World Class Business Coaching, Training, and Development Programs designed for business owners and entrepreneurs just like you...

We recognise that all businesses are different, as are the people that build, own and run them so we have a range of products and programs that will help, inspire and support you – whatever stage of development your business is at...

You can register for our newsletter, check out David's latest blog and even download documents and templates from our website at www.resultsrulesok.com

If you'd like to come along to an event – either to join one of our Webinars or participate in a Workshop or Seminar – visit our website www.resultsrulesok.com to find our full schedule of events.

David is offers a limited number of FREE **Business Strategy Sessions** for qualifying businesses, to arrange a meeting or discussion with David, simply got to www.resultsrulesok.com, scroll down and press the **"Book Free Session with David"** button...

Our USP is our people, our delivery, the results our Clients achieve and our philosophy of Fun in Life and in Business. We are a growing profitable business, and we believe in making contributions to charity and causes that are aligned with our values.

David's unique experience, background and passion for adding value to the business and personal lives of others have enabled him to become not only a top Business Coach, but an accomplished Speaker and Author. Having worked in 21 countries so far, his presentations and key note presentations are compelling, informative and fun and his books reflect his knowledge and personality…

David's best-selling business book available now…

Your Business Rules OK

If you have got this far then maybe we should talk…!

Contact Us;
Web – www.resultsrulesok.com
Email – info@resultsrulesok.com

Other Books by David Holland now available

Your Business Rules OK

Only Read at 4am

Would you like Fries with That?

Is Business Coaching Hornswoggle

Learning How to Fly

Unlucky for Some

The Case of the Ego in the Corner

The YOU Tree

Lights, Camera, Action

Contrary to Popular Belief

Every Day in Every Way, I'm Getting Better & Better

Success Matters

Success Rules OK

Scared of the Dark?

Leads United

Selling & Closing

The Franchise Connection

The Professional Tarot

Goals, Objectives and Precession

How to Surf the Tsunami...

Strength in Numbers....

Dutch Courage...

Negotiating Success

The 9 Rules

Drumming and the Art of Business Maintenance

The 5 P's Professionals need to know

Growing Pains

Fractional Thinking

Customers for Life

Presenting Excellence

Goals Suck

Excellence is a Real Pitch

Questions from your Favourite Teenager

The Time that People Forgot

The How 2 Series

Life Rules Ok

David is a rare pearl in the world of today - he has a human approach to life's problems - he tells it how it is and gives you the toolkit to move forwards and to seek your own solutions. He genuinely cares about the people he works with. Working with him and his team has been an extremely positive experience.
Nicola O'Neill Luxembourg

David Holland (aka Dutch) is the best coach I've ever worked with. Not only did he help train me in coaching but he walked with me during the most difficult period in my professional career and helped me get back up after I had been knocked down. I will always love this man and my only complaint is he no longer lives in the U.S.
Josh McGinnis USA

I have had the pleasure to work with David over the past 6 months and he is truly an asset to anyone looking to grow and develop themselves, whether that be on a personal or professional basis.

David has a vast catalogue of coaching expertise and a very diverse client list. This adds up to him adding value to any conversation and tell humorous, personal anecdotes along the way.

David's gentle, personable demeanour belies his continuous drive for results and he is always on hand to make sure you follow through on what you've agreed to do.

I have loved working with David; my new business would not be where it is today were it not for his guidance and continued support. Thank you, David...!

Allison Langley Butnick UK

www.resultsrulesok.com